7/09

Following Directions

Grades 5–6

Written by
Linda Schwartz

Illustrated by
Mark Mason

Editor: Pam VanBlaricum
Illustrator: Mark Mason
Designer: Eric Larson, Studio E Books
Cover Artist: Kimberly Schamber
Cover Designer: Barbara Peterson
Art Director: Tom Cochrane
Project Director: Linda Schwartz

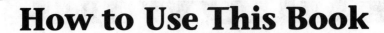

How to Use This Book

The activities in this book will give your students practice and competence in following written directions, step-by-step directions, and oral directions. In addition to the worksheets, the only supplies needed are pencils and crayons. The first section of the book contains written directions for your students to follow. In the second section, written step-by-step directions and illustrations instruct students to draw simple pictures. In the third section, you read a set of directions to your students while they listen and do the work on their activity sheets. Pages in the book may be used in any order.

Contents

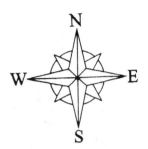

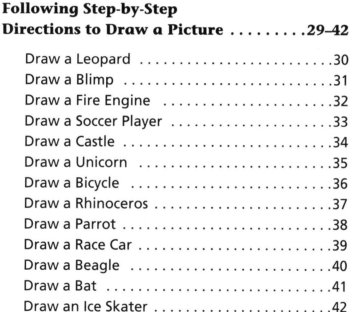

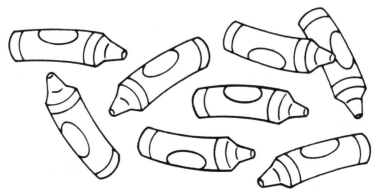

Contents (continued)

Following Written Directions

Name: _____

Graph a Giraffe

Using a ruler and the grid on page 7, draw straight lines to connect the grid points below in the order given. You will create a picture of a giraffe. The first lines have been drawn for you.

1.	W-11	W-5	V-5	T-10	U-11	
2.	U-11	U-22	P-27	O-23	V-2	
3.	V-2	T-2	Q-13	N-21	M-22	
4.	M-22	L-13	M-2	K-2	K-23	
5.	K-23	I-23	G-23	F-19	C-12	
6.	C-12	D-2	B-2	B-14	C-16	C-30
7.	I-23	I-19	F-12	G-2	E-2	E-14 F-19
8.	C-30	N-35	X-23	W-11		

Following Directions • 5–6 ©2004 Creative Teaching Press

Name: _____

Graph a Giraffe

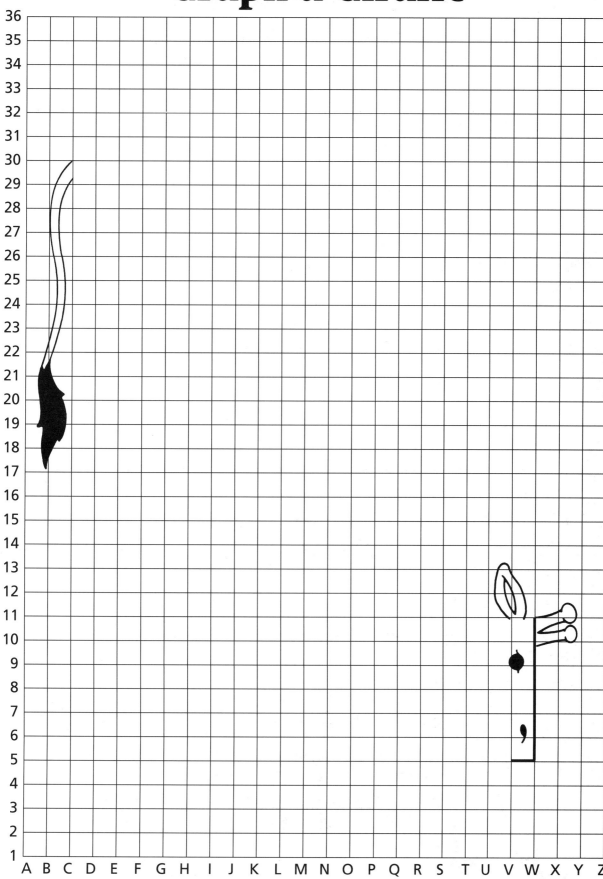

Make a Mantis

Using a ruler and the grid on page 9, draw straight lines to connect the grid points below in the order given. You will create a picture of a praying mantis. The first lines have been drawn for you.

1. K-27   P-22   U-27

2. N-22   R-22   P-19   N-22

3. O-19   Q-19   Q-13   O-13   O-19

4. O-13   M-14   C-14   G-12   M-12   O-13

5. E-13   B-13   E-10   M-10   Q-13

6. D-18   C-19   F-23   J-18   O-18

7. Q-18   V-18   V-24   Y-19   X-18

8. F-23   H-19   J-18   N-17   O-18

9. Q-18   R-17   V-18   W-19   V-24

10. M-10   E-12   B-2

11. M-10   G-16   G-2

12. M-10   S-12   U-2

13. M-10   U-16   Y-2

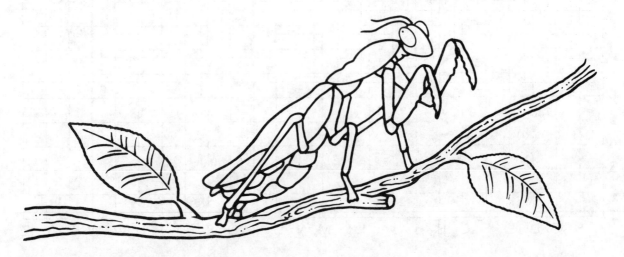

Following Directions • 5–6   ©2004 Creative Teaching Press

Make a Mantis

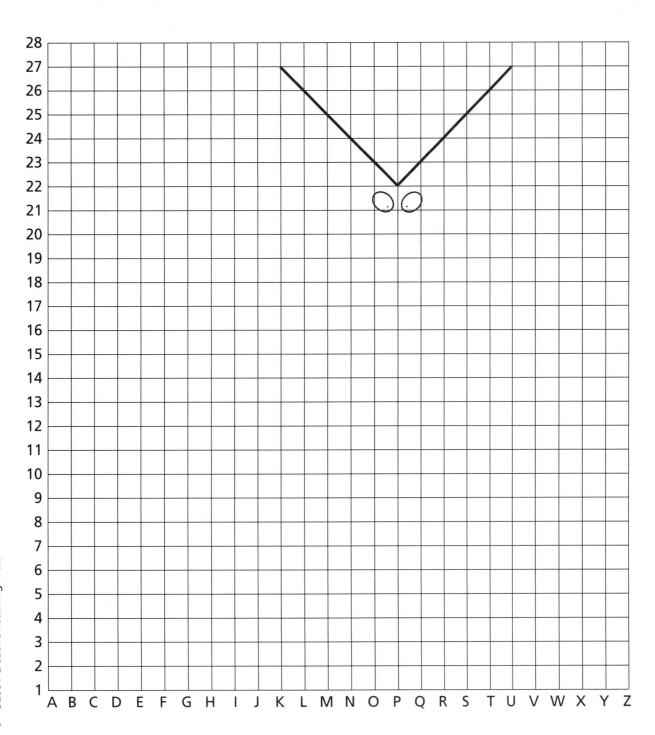

Animal Groups

Follow the directions to find the names of these animal groups. Write the letters on the numbered lines on page 11. Draw an X in each box when you complete the direction. The first one has been done for you.

[X] On line 4, write the 3rd letter of the word HAWK.

[ ] On line 41, write the 5th letter of the word CHIPMUNK.

[ ] On line 5, write the 3rd letter of the word HEDGEHOG.

[ ] On lines 30 and 40, write the 1st letter of the word YAK.

[ ] On line 38, write the 4th letter of the word WOLVERINE.

[ ] On line 15, write the 1st letter of the word FISH.

[ ] On line 35, write the 4th letter of the word ELEPHANT.

[ ] On line 29, write the 8th letter of the word PORCUPINE.

[ ] On lines 10 and 42, write the 6th letter of the word OPOSSUM.

[ ] On lines 14 and 20, write the 5th letter of the word ZEBRA.

[ ] On lines 9 and 12, write the 9th letter of the word WOODCHUCK.

[ ] On lines 16, 31, and 44, write the 8th letter of the word HIPPOPOTAMUS.

[ ] On lines 2, 11, 23, and 27, write the 6th letter of the word WEASEL.

[ ] On lines 6, 17, 24, 39, and 45, write the 7th letter of the word SQUIRREL.

[ ] On lines 7, 13, 18, 32, and 46, write the 6th letter of the word KANGAROO.

[ ] On lines 1, 25, and 36, write the 2nd letter of the word OCELOT.

[ ] On lines 3, 26, 28, 33, 34, and 37, write the 5th letter of the word MARMOSET.

[ ] On lines 8 and 43, write the 6th letter of the word WALRUS.

[ ] On lines 19, 21, and 22, write the 7th letter of the word WARTHOG.

Following Directions • 5–6   ©2004 Creative Teaching Press

Animal Groups

a __ __ __ W __ __ __ of cats
   1 2 3 4 5 6 7

a __ __ __ __ __ of foxes
   8 9 10 11 12

a __ __ __ __ __ __ of turkeys
   13 14 15 16 17 18

a __ __ __ __ __ __ of geese
   19 20 21 22 23 24

a __ __ __ __ __ __ of rabbits
   25 26 27 28 29 30

a __ __ __ __ __ of kangaroos
   31 32 33 34 35

a __ __ __ __ __ of partridges
   36 37 38 39 40

a __ __ __ __ __ __ of peacocks
   41 42 43 44 45 46

Animal Offspring

Follow the directions to find the names of these animal offspring. Write the letters on the numbered lines on page 13. Draw an X in each box when you complete the direction. The first one has been done for you.

[X] On line 13, write the 1st letter of the word FLAMINGO.

[ ] On line 33, write the 2nd letter of the word DUCK.

[ ] On line 20, write the 7th letter of the word SPARROW.

[ ] On line 38, write the 4th letter of the word GOOSE.

[ ] On line 9, write the 4th letter of the word DONKEY.

[ ] On line 1, write the 1st letter of the word JAY.

[ ] On lines 4 and 26, write the 6th letter of the word TURKEY.

[ ] On lines 24 and 31, write the 7th letter of the word ANTELOPE.

[ ] On lines 7 and 40, write the 3rd letter of the word CHICKEN.

[ ] On lines 28 and 41, write the 7th letter of the word ELEPHANT.

[ ] On lines 11 and 15, write the 5th letter of the word BOBCAT.

[ ] On lines 6 and 21, write the 1st letter of the word HAWK.

[ ] On lines 16, 27, 36, and 42, write the 1st letter of the word GIRAFFE.

[ ] On lines 2, 32, and 37, write the 5th letter of the word PEACOCK.

[ ] On lines 19, 30, and 35, write the 8th letter of the word HIPPOPOTAMUS.

[ ] On lines 12, 17, 23, 34, and 39, write the 8th letter of the word SQUIRREL.

[ ] On lines 3, 14, 18, 22, and 29, write the 5th letter of the word WHALE.

[ ] On lines 5, 8, 10, and 25, write the 6th letter of the word RHINOCEROS.

Following Directions • 5–6 ©2004 Creative Teaching Press

Name: _____

Animal Offspring

kangaroo: __ __ __ __
          1 2 3 4

ostrich: __ __ __ __ __
         5 6 7 8 9

rhinoceros: __ __ __ **F**
            10 11 12 13

eagle: __ __ __ __ __ __
       14 15 16 17 18 19

otter: __ __ __ __ __
       20 21 22 23 24

swan: __ __ __ __ __ __
      25 26 27 28 29 30

turkey: __ __ __ __ __
        31 32 33 34 35

goose: __ __ __ __ __ __ __
       36 37 38 39 40 41 42

Name the Inventor

Follow the directions to find the names of these famous inventors. Write the letters on the numbered lines on page 15. Draw an X in each box when you complete the direction. The first one has been done for you.

[X] On line 19, write the 2nd letter of the word AUTOMOBILE.

[ ] On line 18, write the 1st letter of the first word in COTTON GIN.

[ ] On lines 21 and 31, write the 6th letter of the word ELEVATOR.

[ ] On lines 3 and 8, write the 7th letter of the word TELEPHONE.

[ ] On line 45, write the 1st letter of the second word in ELECTRIC FAN.

[ ] On lines 25 and 40, write the 1st letter of the first word in JUMPER CABLE.

[ ] On lines 14, 34, and 50, write the 3rd letter of the word TELEGRAPH.

[ ] On lines 12 and 36, write the 7th letter of the word BATTERY.

[ ] On line 37, write the 1st letter of the second word in ELEVATOR BRAKE.

[ ] On lines 2 and 13, write the 5th letter of the word DIRIGIBLE.

[ ] On lines 15, 28, 35, and 38, write the 3rd letter of the word STEAMBOAT.

[ ] On lines 1, 6, 22, 43, and 51, write the 4th letter of the word CYLINDER.

[ ] On lines 4, 9, 20, 33, and 46, write the 2nd letter of the word TRANSISTOR.

[ ] On lines 7, 11, and 49, write the 4th letter of the second word in AIR BRAKE.

[ ] On lines 27 and 42, write the 1st letter of the first word in MORSE CODE.

[ ] On lines 16, 17, 39, 44, 48, and 52, write the 3rd letter of the word PENICILLIN.

[ ] On lines 5, 10, 23, 24, 29, and 30, write the 1st letter of the first word in SEWING MACHINE.

[ ] On lines 26, 32, 41, and 47, write the 2nd letter of the word CAMERA.

Following Directions • 5–6 ©2004 Creative Teaching Press

Name the Inventor

$\overline{}_{1}$ $\overline{}_{2}$ $\overline{}_{3}$ $\overline{}_{4}$ $\overline{}_{5}$ $\overline{}_{6}$ $\overline{}_{7}$ $\overline{}_{8}$ $\overline{}_{9}$ $\overline{}_{10}$ $\overline{}_{11}$ $\overline{}_{12}$

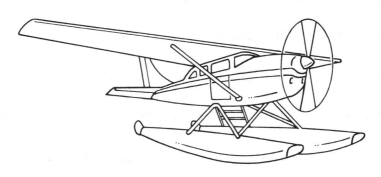

U

$\overline{}_{13}$ $\overline{}_{14}$ $\overline{}_{15}$ $\overline{}_{16}$ $\overline{}_{17}$ $\overline{}_{18}$ $\overline{U}_{19}$ $\overline{}_{20}$ $\overline{}_{21}$ $\overline{}_{22}$ $\overline{}_{23}$ $\overline{}_{24}$

$\overline{}_{25}$ $\overline{}_{26}$ $\overline{}_{27}$ $\overline{}_{28}$ $\overline{}_{29}$ $\overline{}_{30}$ $\overline{}_{31}$ $\overline{}_{32}$ $\overline{}_{33}$ $\overline{}_{34}$ $\overline{}_{35}$ $\overline{}_{36}$

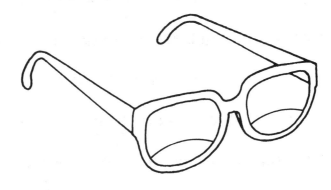

$\overline{}_{37}$ $\overline{}_{38}$ $\overline{}_{39}$ $\overline{}_{40}$ $\overline{}_{41}$ $\overline{}_{42}$ $\overline{}_{43}$ $\overline{}_{44}$ $\overline{}_{45}$ $\overline{}_{46}$ $\overline{}_{47}$ $\overline{}_{48}$ $\overline{}_{49}$ $\overline{}_{50}$ $\overline{}_{51}$ $\overline{}_{52}$

State Safari

Use the clues below to eliminate the names of the states listed on page 17. The first one has been done for you. (In most cases, you will eliminate more than one state at a time.) Draw an X in the box as you eliminate each state until the name of only one is left. If you have followed directions correctly, you will discover the answer to this question:

Which was the first state to be admitted to the Union?

1. The state's name does *not* have two of the same vowels right next to each other.

2. There is no letter B in the name of the state.

3. The state's name does not begin and end with the same letter.

4. There is no letter G in the name of the state.

5. The last two letters in the state's name do not spell the words "as" or "is."

6. The last two letters in the state's name do not spell the word "in."

7. The state's name does not have two of the same consonants right next to each other.

8. The state's name does not end in the letter O.

9. The names "Mary," "Ken," and "Louis" do not appear at the beginning of the state's name.

10. The word "new" does not appear in the state's name.

11. The state's name is not made up of two words.

12. The state's name has more than four letters.

13. There are more than two vowels in the state's name.

14. The letter A appears two times in the state's name.

15. There is no letter T or V in the state's name.

16. The last letter of the state's name is not an A.

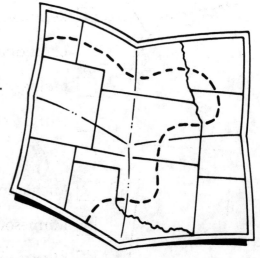

Following Directions • 5–6 ©2004 Creative Teaching Press

The name of the state is _____.

Name: _____

State Safari

☐ Alabama	☐ Montana
☐ Alaska	☐ Nebraska
☐ Arizona	☐ Nevada
☐ Arkansas	☐ New Hampshire
☐ California	☐ New Jersey
☐ Colorado	☐ New Mexico
☐ Connecticut	☐ New York
☐ Delaware	☐ North Carolina
☐ Florida	☐ North Dakota
☐ Georgia	☐ Ohio
☒ Hawaii	☐ Oklahoma
☐ Idaho	☐ Oregon
☐ Illinois	☐ Pennsylvania
☐ Indiana	☐ Rhode Island
☐ Iowa	☐ South Carolina
☐ Kansas	☐ South Dakota
☐ Kentucky	☒ Tennessee
☐ Louisiana	☐ Texas
☐ Maine	☐ Utah
☐ Maryland	☐ Vermont
☐ Massachusetts	☐ Virginia
☐ Michigan	☐ Washington
☐ Minnesota	☐ West Virginia
☐ Mississippi	☐ Wisconsin
☐ Missouri	☐ Wyoming

Following Directions • 5–6 ©2004 Creative Teaching Press

Following Written Directions • 17

Name: _____

Name the President

Use the clues below to cross off and eliminate the names of the United States presidents listed on page 19. In most cases, you will eliminate more than one president's name at a time. If you have followed directions correctly, you will discover the answer to this question:

Which United States president is pictured on a $5,000 bill?

1. The president's first and last names do not start with the same letter.

2. The president's last name does not have two of the same letters right next to each other.

3. The president's last name does not have exactly four letters.

4. The president's first name does not begin with the letter A.

5. Part of the president's name is not the name of a vehicle that rhymes with *man*.

6. The last four letters of the president's last name do not spell the word *land*.

7. The president's first name does not end with the letter Y.

8. The president's last name does not end with a vowel.

9. There is no letter R in the president's last name.

10. The president's last name does not have exactly five letters.

11. There is no letter U or L in the president's last name.

12. The letters G and T do not appear next to each other in the president's last name.

13. There is no letter Y in the president's first name.

The president who is pictured on the $5000 bill is _____ .

Following Directions • 5–6 ©2004 Creative Teaching Press

Name the President

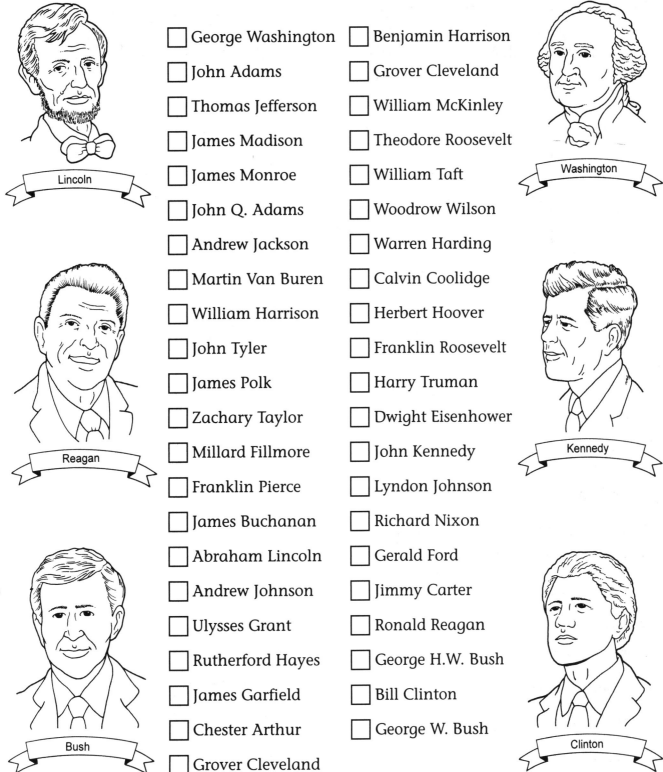

Lincoln

Reagan

Bush

Washington

Kennedy

Clinton

- [ ] George Washington
- [ ] John Adams
- [ ] Thomas Jefferson
- [ ] James Madison
- [ ] James Monroe
- [ ] John Q. Adams
- [ ] Andrew Jackson
- [ ] Martin Van Buren
- [ ] William Harrison
- [ ] John Tyler
- [ ] James Polk
- [ ] Zachary Taylor
- [ ] Millard Fillmore
- [ ] Franklin Pierce
- [ ] James Buchanan
- [ ] Abraham Lincoln
- [ ] Andrew Johnson
- [ ] Ulysses Grant
- [ ] Rutherford Hayes
- [ ] James Garfield
- [ ] Chester Arthur
- [ ] Grover Cleveland

- [ ] Benjamin Harrison
- [ ] Grover Cleveland
- [ ] William McKinley
- [ ] Theodore Roosevelt
- [ ] William Taft
- [ ] Woodrow Wilson
- [ ] Warren Harding
- [ ] Calvin Coolidge
- [ ] Herbert Hoover
- [ ] Franklin Roosevelt
- [ ] Harry Truman
- [ ] Dwight Eisenhower
- [ ] John Kennedy
- [ ] Lyndon Johnson
- [ ] Richard Nixon
- [ ] Gerald Ford
- [ ] Jimmy Carter
- [ ] Ronald Reagan
- [ ] George H.W. Bush
- [ ] Bill Clinton
- [ ] George W. Bush

NOTE: Grover Cleveland served two non-consecutive terms. Be sure to cross his name off twice.

Geometry Goulash

Follow the directions below using the worksheet on page 21.

1. Write the letter that is not in any of the shapes. _____

2. Write the letter that is only in the oval. _____

3. Write the letter that is only in the oval and circle. _____

4. Write the letter that is only in the semicircle. _____

5. Write the letter that is only in the oval and the rectangle. _____

6. Write the letter that is only in the square and rectangle. _____

7. Write the letter that is only in the semicircle and circle. _____

8. Write the letter that is in the oval, the circle, and the rectangle. _____

9. Write the letter that is in the semicircle, the rectangle, and the circle. _____

10. Write the letters that are only in the triangle. _____

11. Write the letters that are only in the rectangle. _____

12. Write the letter that is only in the circle and the rectangle. _____

13. Write the letters that are in the oval but not in the rectangle. _____

14. Write the letter that is only in the square, the circle, and the rectangle. _____

15. Write the letters that are in the rectangle but not in the square or circle. _____

16. Write the letters that are only in the square. _____

17. Write the letters that are in the rectangle but not in the oval or semicircle. _____

18. Write the letters that are in the circle but not in the square or semicircle. _____

Following Directions • 5–6 ©2004 Creative Teaching Press

Geometry Goulash

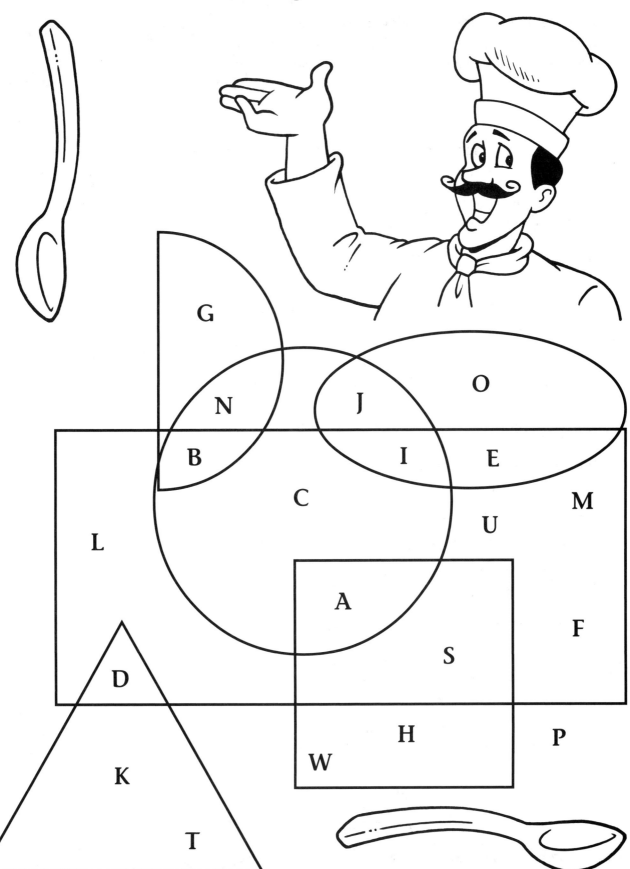

Name: _____

What's for Dinner?

Alphabetize these words and follow the directions to find out what's for dinner. Use the worksheet on page 23. The first one has been done for you.

1. If *pizza* comes before *pie* in the dictionary, write the number 7 in the box under the fish. If not, write the number 12 in the box.

2. If *cheese* comes before *chicken*, write the number 8 in the box under the macaroni and cheese. If not, write the number 2 in the box.

3. If *cherry* comes before *chestnut*, write the number 3 in the box under the hamburger. If not, write the number 4 in the box.

4. If *potato* comes before *porridge*, write the number 2 in the box under the chicken. If not, write the number 5 in the box.

5. If *sandwich* comes after *salmon*, write the number 2 in the box under the salad. If not, write the number 10 in the box.

6. If *peach* comes after *pecan*, write the number 4 in the box under the spaghetti. If not, write the number 7 in the box.

7. If *broccoli* comes before *broth*, write the number 1 in the box under the taco. If not, write the number 5 in the box.

8. If *turkey* comes before *tuna*, write the number 9 in the box under the steak. If not, write the number 6 in the box.

9. If *pickle* comes after *pizza*, write the number 12 in the box under the stew. If not, write the number 11 in the box.

10. If *cheddar* comes before *cheese*, write the number 9 in the box under the pizza. If not, write the number 7 in the box.

11. If *sour cream* comes after *soup*, write the number 4 in the box under the ham. If not, write the number 3 in the box.

12. If *strawberry* comes after *string bean*, write the number 14 in the box under the turkey. If not, write the number 10 in the box.

To find out what's for dinner, add the numbers in the boxes under the steak and ham.
Write this sum on the line: _____

What food has this number and is being served for dinner? _____

Following Directions • 5–6   ©2004 Creative Teaching Press

What's for Dinner?

Following Directions • 5–6 ©2004 Creative Teaching Press

Mall Maze

Alphabetize these words and follow the directions on page 25 as you go through the mall. The first one has been done for you.

1. If *shoe* comes before *slipper* in the dictionary, write the number 9 in the Shoe Salon. If not, write the number 5 in this store.

2. If *emerald* comes before *diamond*, write the number 2 in Jewels by Jenna. If not, write the number 4 in this store.

3. If *hot dog* comes before *hamburger*, write the number 3 in Tutti's Cafe. If not, write the number 1 in this restaurant.

4. If *basketball* comes before *baseball*, write the number 7 in Sal's Sporting Goods. If not, write the number 8.

5. If *classical* comes after *country*, write the number 15 in the Music Man. If not, write the number 5.

6. If *licorice* comes before *lollipop*, write the number 11 in The Sweet Shop. If not, write the number 6.

7. If *bedding* comes before *bedspread*, write the number 17 in The Home Store. If not, write the number 2.

8. If *fable* comes after *fantasy*, write the number 5 in the Book Barn. If not, write the number 12.

9. If *narcissus* comes before *nasturtium*, write the number 3 in Flora's Flower Cart. If not, write the number 2.

10. If *Dalmatian* comes before *dachshund*, write the number 5 in Pets and More. If not, write the number 7.

11. If *card* comes after *candle*, write the number 6 in Card and Gift Shop. If not, write the number 10.

12. If *shirt* comes before *skirt*, write the number 14 in Jay Company Department Store. If not, write the number 6.

13. If *rocking horse* comes before *rocket*, write the number 9 in the Kids' Play Area. If not, write the number 10.

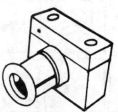

14. If *photographer* comes after *photography*, write the number 7 in the Photo Gallery. If not, write the number 13.

Add the numbers in Music Man, The Home Store, and Book Barn.

Write the sum: _____

Following Directions • 5–6 ©2004 Creative Teaching Press

Mall Maze

Best in Show

Which dog on page 27 won Best in Show? To find out, read the
judges' comments and cross off one dog at a time until only one is left.

The dog that won
does not have exactly
five letters in its name.

The dog that won
does not have a name
that is a compound word.

The winning dog does not
have a name that rhymes
with the word *noodle*.

The winning dog does not have
a name with two identical
consonants in the middle.

The name of the winning dog
does not have exactly two *u*'s
in its name.

The dog that won does not
have exactly fifteen letters
in its name.

The last five letters of the
winning dog do not spell the
name of a bird.

The winning dog does not have
a name that starts and ends
with consonants.

The dog the judges picked for Best in Show was the _____.

Following Directions • 5–6   ©2004 Creative Teaching Press

Best in Show

Poodle

Cocker Spaniel

Golden Retriever

Chihuahua

Australian Shepherd

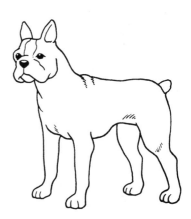

Boxer

Collie

Bloodhound

Beagle

Name: _____

The Magic Number

Find the magic number by following the directions
and crossing off one number at a time until only one is left.

341,036   302,186

740,215   435,501

812,549   510,362

698,126   255,457

105,328

CLUES

1. The magic number does not have three 5s. Find and cross off the number with three 5s.
2. The magic number does not have more than one 3.
3. The sum of the last two digits of the magic number does not equal 10.
4. The magic number does not start and end with an odd number.
5. The magic number does not have two of the same number next to each other in the middle.
6. The sum of the first and last digit of the magic number is not 17.
7. The magic number does not start and end with the same number.
8. The sum of the first and last digit of the magic number is not 7.

The magic number is _____ .

Following Directions • 5–6 ©2004 Creative Teaching Press

Following Step-By-Step Directions to Draw a Picture

Draw a Leopard

#1

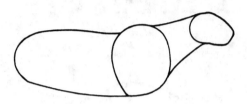

Draw the body, neck, and head of the leopard.

#2

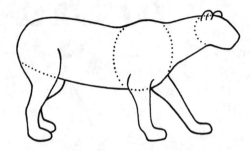

Draw the four legs. Add the ears.
Erase the dotted lines.

#3

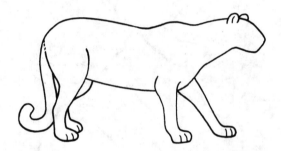

Draw a tail on the leopard. Add paws on each
foot. Erase the dotted line.

#4

Draw a nose, mouth, and eye on the head.
Draw spots on the leopard.

Draw your leopard here. Add trees to shade your leopard.

Following Directions • 5–6 ©2004 Creative Teaching Press

Draw a Blimp

#1

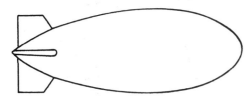

Draw the body of the blimp.
Add the rudder and tail.

#2

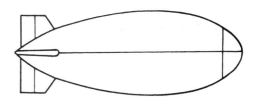

Draw a line dividing the body in half as shown.
Add details on the body and tail.

#3

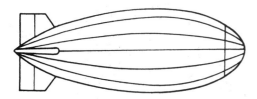

Draw curved lines on the body.

#4

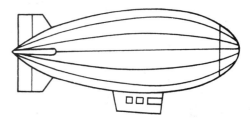

Draw a gondola with three windows
under the blimp.

Draw your blimp here. Draw clouds in the sky around your blimp.

Draw a Fire Engine

#1

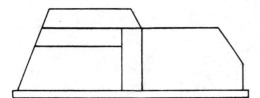

Draw the body of the fire engine as shown.

#2

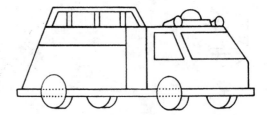

Add the ladder and sirens. Draw four wheels and two windows. Erase the dotted lines.

#3

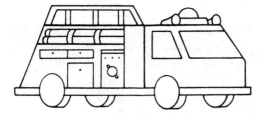

Add the hoses and other details to the side of the fire engine as shown.

#4

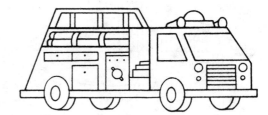

Draw stairs, a front grill, and headlights. Draw smaller circles inside the two right tires.

Draw your fire engine here. In the background, draw a building on fire.

Following Directions • 5–6 ©2004 Creative Teaching Press

Name: _____

Draw a Soccer Player

#1

Draw the head, neck, and body. Draw lines as shown for the start of the arms and legs.

#2

Complete the arms and legs. Draw shorts on the soccer player. Erase the dotted lines.

#3

Draw hands and shoes.
Add a collar and details to the shirt.

#4

Erase the dotted line. Draw hair and facial features. Draw socks on the soccer player.

Draw your soccer player here. Draw a soccer ball by the boy's feet.

Draw a Castle

#1

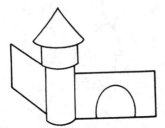

Draw the front and side of the castle with the corner tower. Add a door.

#2

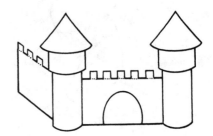

Add the tower on the right. Add the crenels on top of the castle wall. Erase the dotted lines.

#3

Add the two towers in the back of the castle.

#4

Draw the other two walls. On each tower, add a window and a flag. Draw a gate on the door.

Draw your castle here. Add a moat filled with water around your castle.

Following Directions • 5–6   ©2004 Creative Teaching Press

Name: _____

Draw a Unicorn

#1

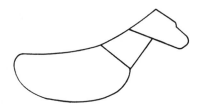

Draw the head, neck, and body of the unicorn.

#2

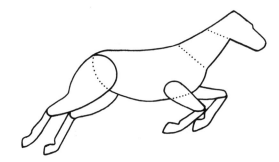

Draw the front and back legs.
Erase the dotted lines.

#3

Draw a mane, tail, and ear. Add a curve to the head as shown. Erase the dotted lines.

#4

Draw an eye, nose, mouth, horn, and hooves.

Draw your unicorn here. Draw a rainbow behind your unicorn.

Draw a Bicycle

#1

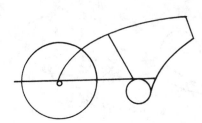

Draw the frame and back wheel.

#2

Add the front wheel, seat, and handlebars.
Complete the frame.

#3

Draw inner circles for the tires as shown.
Add the pedals and chain.

#4

Draw spokes and fenders on each wheel.

Draw your bicycle here. Draw a bike path lined with flowers for your bicycle.

Draw a Rhinoceros

#1

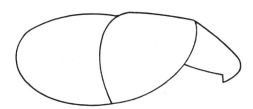

Draw the head and body of the rhinoceros.

#2

Add a curved line for the jaw.
Add four legs and feet. Erase the dotted lines.

#3

Draw details on the body. Add ears, a horn,
a mouth, and a tail. Erase the dotted lines.

#4

Draw an eye, eyebrow, and nostril.

Draw your rhinoceros here. Add a river for your rhino to wade in.

Following Directions • 5–6 ©2004 Creative Teaching Press

Draw a Parrot

#1

Draw the body, tail, and wings.

#2

Add feathers to the wings and tail.
Draw a beak and feet. Erase the dotted lines.

#3

Draw details on the body as shown.
Erase the dotted line.

#4

Draw a perch for the parrot. Add an eye.

Draw your parrot on the left. Draw another parrot on the right,
so that they can talk to each other.

Following Directions • 5–6 ©2004 Creative Teaching Press

Name: _____

Draw a Race Car

#1

Draw the body of the car as shown.

#2

Add a spoiler to the back of the car.
Add details to the car as shown.

#3

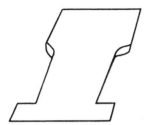

Draw the four wheels and front axles.

#4

Draw a steering wheel.
Add details to the wheels as shown.

Draw your race car here. Draw the head of a race car driver sitting behind the wheel.

Draw a Beagle

#1

Draw the head, neck, and body of the beagle.

#2

Draw the four legs. Erase the dotted lines.

#3

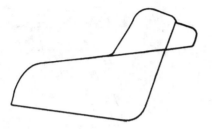

Draw an ear, an eye, a nose, and a mouth.

#4

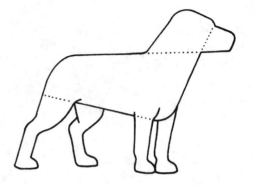

Draw a tail. Add spots on the beagle's body and tail.

Draw your beagle here. Draw a bone for your dog to eat.

Following Directions • 5–6 ©2004 Creative Teaching Press

Draw a Bat

#1

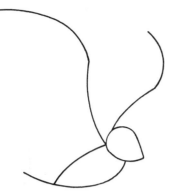

Draw the head and body of the bat.
Draw the outline of the wings as shown.

#2

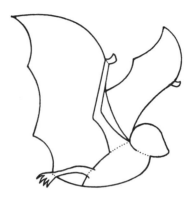

Complete the wings as shown. Add arms
and the right leg. Erase the dotted lines.

#3

Draw ears on the bat's head. Add details to
the wings as shown. Erase the dotted line.

#4

Add an eye, a nose, and a mouth.

Draw your bat here. Draw a moon and stars in the night sky behind your bat.

Draw an Ice Skater

#1

Draw the head, neck, upper body, and arms.
Draw lines as shown for the start of the legs.

#2

Complete the legs. Add skates and the skirt.
Erase the dotted lines.

#3

Add the skater's hands and hair.
Erase the dotted lines.

#4

Draw the skater's facial features.
Add lines to show the skater's motion.

Draw your ice skater here. Add a pond and winter background for your skater.

Following Directions • 5–6   ©2004 Creative Teaching Press

Following Oral Directions

Name: _____

Oral Directions to Be Read by the Teacher

To the Teacher
Be sure each student has the appropriate activity sheet, a pencil, and crayons. Ask students to listen very carefully, because you will read each direction only once. They are to listen and do only what you tell them to do. Read each step in the directions slowly and clearly. Pause long enough after each step to give students time to complete the steps you've read, but don't let the pace drag. Do not repeat any of the directions.

Page 51: Kentucky Towns
The map on your work sheet shows some of the towns in the state of Kentucky. Follow the directions that I read to you.

1. Find Dog Walk and Drip Rock. Underline the one that is farther north.
2. Draw a small pyramid next to Egypt.
3. Circle the names that begin with the letter B.
4. Write the letter V by the names that end with "ville."
5. Draw a bone under Marrowbone.
6. Draw an X under each word containing the letter X.
7. Draw a square around the shortest name.
8. Draw a paw print by the word dog and another by the word cat.
9. Make a dotted line from English to London.
10. Draw a flower next to Honeybee.
11. Draw a stoplight next to Lucky Stop.
12. Draw a pine tree next to Yosemite.
13. Draw a snowman next to Snow.
14. Draw a triangle connecting Maud, Zoe, and Olga.
15. Next to Salt Gum, draw the face of someone sticking out his or her tongue.

Following Directions • 5–6   ©2004 Creative Teaching Press

Oral Directions to Be Read by the Teacher

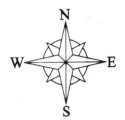

Page 52: Western Quest

I am going to read the names of different western towns. Follow the directions, and write a name of a town in the state where it belongs. If you have followed directions, you should have the names of two towns in each state.

1. The town of *Weed* is located along the Pacific Ocean in the state between Oregon and Arizona. Write the name Weed in this state.
2. The town of *Fishtail* is found in the state north of Wyoming. Write the name Fishtail in this state.
3. Beautiful *Bluebell* is found in the state west of Colorado. Write the name Bluebell in this state.
4. *Dusty* is in the state bordered by Idaho and Oregon. Write the name Dusty in this state.
5. *Pep* and *House* are found in the state directly south of Colorado. Write the names Pep and House in this state.
6. The old town of *Fossil* is found in the state south of Washington. Write the name Fossil in this state.
7. Where can you find the town of *Blue*? In the state just south of the state where Bluebell is found. Write the name Blue in this state.
8. To find the town of *Santa*, go to the state north of Nevada and Utah. Write the name Santa in this state.
9. The town of *Elk* is found in the state southwest of Nevada. Write the name Elk in this state.
10. Are you looking for *Bill*? That town can be found in the state northeast of Utah. Write the name Bill in this state.
11. *Steamboat* and *Stagecoach* are both found in the state directly west of Utah. Write the names Steamboat and Stagecoach in this state.
12. Where is *George*? It's in the state north of Oregon. Write the name George in this state.
13. The little town of *Why* is in the same state as Blue. Write the name Why in this state.
14. *Sandy* is in the state surrounded by Idaho, Wyoming, Colorado, New Mexico, Arizona, and Nevada. Write the name Sandy in this state.
15. The western town of *Rifle* is in the state directly east of Utah. Write the name Rifle in this state.
16. The little town of *Riddle* is in the same state as Santa. Write the name Riddle in this state.
17. The remote town of *Remote* is in the state directly south of Washington. Write the name Remote in this state.
18. *Pony* is found in the state north of Idaho and Wyoming. Write the name Pony in this state.
19. The town of *Story* is in the state between Montana and Colorado. Write the name Story in this state.
20. Brush the dust off your map to find the tiny town of *Brush* in the state just north of New Mexico. Write the name Brush in this state.

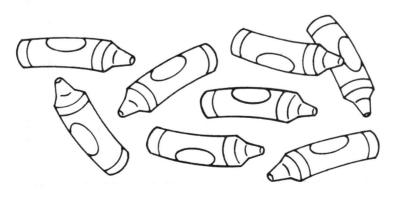

Name: _____

Oral Directions to Be Read by the Teacher

Page 54: North, South, East, and West

Use the map of the United States on page 53 to help you respond to these directions.

1. On line #1, write the name of the state that is directly east of New Hampshire.
2. On line #2, write the name of the state that is directly west of Colorado.
3. On line #3, write the name of the state that is directly south of South Dakota.
4. On line #4, write the name of the state that is directly north of Wyoming.
5. On line #5, write the name of the state that is directly east of Tennessee.
6. On line #6, write the name of the state that is directly south of Georgia.
7. On line #7, write the name of the state that is directly west of Utah.
8. On line #8, write the name of the state that is directly east of Kansas.
9. On line #9, write the name of the state that is directly north of Pennsylvania.
10. On line #10, write the name of the state that is directly south of Wisconsin.
11. On line #11, write the name of the state that is directly west of Texas.
12. On line #12, write the name of the state that is directly north of Mississippi.

Page 55: In-Between States

Use the map of the United States on page 53 to help you respond to these directions.

1. On line #1, write the name of the state that is between Texas and Kansas.
2. On line #2, write the name of the state that is between North Dakota and Nebraska.
3. On line #3, write the name of the state that is between Illinois and Ohio.
4. On line #4, write the name of the state that is between Georgia and Mississippi.
5. On line #5, write the name of the state that is between Minnesota and Missouri.
6. On line #6, write the name of the state that is between Vermont and Connecticut.
7. On line #7, write the name of the state that is between Washington and Montana.
8. On line #8, write the name of the state that is between New Mexico and Wyoming.
9. On line #9, write the name of the state that is between Indiana and Pennsylvania.
10. On line #10, write the name of the state that is between North Dakota and Wisconsin.
11. On line #11, write the name of the state that is between Alabama and Louisiana.
12. On line #12, write the name of the state that is between Tennessee and Indiana.

Page 56: Number, Please

Use the map on page 53 to help you respond to these directions. All the questions refer to the contiguous United States only—not Alaska or Hawaii.

1. How many states border Mexico? Write this number on line #8.
2. How many states border the Gulf of Mexico? Write this number on line #11.
3. How many states border the Pacific Ocean? Write this number on line #5.
4. How many states border Minnesota? Write this number on line #1.
5. How many states border Lake Superior? Write this number on line #12.
6. How many states border Lake Ontario? Write this number on line #4.
7. How many states border Lake Michigan? Write this number on line #3.
8. How many states border Canada? Write this number on line #6.
9. How many states border Utah? Write this number on line #2.
10. How many states border Missouri? Write this number on line #9.
11. How many states border South Dakota? Write this number on line #10.
12. How many states border Nebraska? Write this number on line #7.

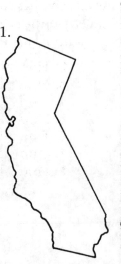

Following Directions • 5–6 ©2004 Creative Teaching Press

Oral Directions to Be Read by the Teacher

Page 57: Hidden Picture #1

Listen to the directions for coloring the picture on your activity sheet. Put your crayon on your desk when you have colored in each step so that I can tell you're ready for the next direction. Wait quietly until your classmates have finished.

1. Find all the shapes with the letter G. Color these shapes green.
2. Find all the shapes with the letter Y. Color these shapes yellow.
3. Find all the shapes with the letter P. Color these shapes purple.
4. Find all the shapes with the letter B. Color these shapes blue.
5. Find all the shapes with the letter O. Color these shapes orange.
6. Find all the shapes with the letter R. Color these shapes red.
7. Find all the shapes with the letters BN. Color these shapes brown.
8. Find all the shapes with the letters BK. Color these shapes black.

Page 58: Hidden Picture #2

Listen to the directions for coloring the picture on your activity sheet. Put your crayon on your desk when you have colored in each step so that I can tell you're ready for the next direction. Wait quietly until your classmates have finished.

1. Find all the shapes with the letter G. Color these shapes green.
2. Find all the shapes with the letter Y. Color these shapes yellow.
3. Find all the shapes with the letter P. Color these shapes purple.
4. Find all the shapes with the letter B. Color these shapes blue.
5. Find all the shapes with the letter O. Color these shapes orange.
6. Find all the shapes with the letter R. Color these shapes red.
7. Find all the shapes with the letters BN. Color these shapes brown.
8. Find all the shapes with the letters BK. Color these shapes black.

Oral Directions to Be Read by the Teacher

Page 59: The Number Game

Pictured on your activity sheet are cards with various numbers. I am going to read clues. Please listen carefully and eliminate one card at a time until only one is left. Each time you eliminate a card, draw an X over the number to cross it off. Let's do the first one together.

1. The number you are looking for is *not* the number of days in a week. (Pause long enough to give students a chance to find the correct answer.) Raise your hand if you knew which card to cross off. If you answered the card with the number 7, you are correct. Did you draw an X over the number 7 to eliminate this card? Now you're on your own as we continue.

2. The number is *not* the number of hours in one day. Cross off this card.
3. The number is *not* the number of states in the United States. Cross off this card.
4. The number is *not* the number of months in a year. Cross off this card.
5. The number is *not* the number of seconds in a minute. Cross off this card.
6. The number is *not* the number of days in a year not counting leap year. Cross off this card.
7. The number is *not* the number of planets in the solar system. Cross off this card.
8. The number is *not* the sum of red and white stripes on the U.S. flag. Cross off this card.
9. The number is *not* the number of degrees in a circle. Cross off this card.
10. The number is *not* the value of Roman numeral V. Cross off this card.
11. The number is *not* the number of feet in a yard. Cross off this card.
12. The number is *not* the value of Roman numeral X. Cross off this card.
13. The number is *not* the number of ounces in a pound. Cross off this card.
14. The number is *not* the number of years in a century. Cross off this card.
15. The number is *not* the number of zeros in a million. Cross off this card.

You should now have one number that has not been crossed off.

This will be the missing number if you have followed directions correctly.

Write the number in the sign the magician is holding.

Following Directions • 5–6 ©2004 Creative Teaching Press

Oral Directions to Be Read by the Teacher

Page 60: Customize the Sport Shoes

Grab your crayons, listen carefully, and follow the directions to customize the sport shoes on page 60. Please put your crayon down when you have completed each direction so I can tell when you're finished and it's time for another direction.

1. Draw three red flowers with green leaves on shoe #8.
2. Draw two blue racing stripes on shoe #4.
3. Draw four yellow stars on shoe #9.
4. Write your first name on shoe #1.
5. Write your favorite number on the side of shoe #6.
6. Draw an orange lightning bolt on shoe #7.
7. Draw purple polka dots on shoe #3.
8. Make shoe #12 red and blue plaid.
9. Draw three interlocking green circles on shoe #10.
10. Draw two palm trees on shoe #2.
11. Write the name of the city where you were born on shoe #11.
12. Create your own original design on shoe #5. It could be a drawing of your favorite food, animal, car, or anything you like!

Page 61: Colorful Crayons

For this activity you will need crayons and the activity sheet on page 61. Please listen and follow the directions as I read them one at a time.

1. Using your red crayon, color the two crayons that contain words that are shades of red.
2. Using your yellow crayon, color the two crayons that contain words that are shades of yellow.
3. Using your purple crayon, color the two crayons that contain words that are shades of purple.
4. Using your orange crayon, color the two crayons that contain words that are shades of orange.
5. Using your green crayon, color the two crayons that contain words that are shades of green.
6. Using your blue crayon, color the two crayons that contain words that are shades of blue.
7. Using your brown crayon, color the two crayons that contain words that are shades of brown.
8. Using your gray crayon, color the two crayons that contain words that are shades of gray. If you do not have a gray crayon, use your black crayon and color the two crayons lightly.
9. Do not color the two crayons that contain words that are shades of white.

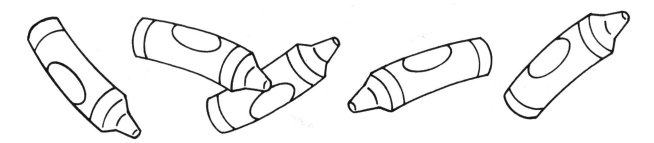

Oral Directions to Be Read by the Teacher

Page 62: Athletes on Parade

I am going to read directions for you to follow on page 62. When asked for a direction such as right or left, I am referring to the athlete who is to *your* right or left as you look at the drawings of the sixteen athletes. Let's do the first one together to be sure you understand.

1. Put the number 16 in the box of the athlete directly to the right of the swimmer. (Pause to give students a chance to follow the direction.) The tennis player is directly to the right of the swimmer. Did you put the #16 on the tennis player? If you put the #16 on any other athlete, please correct your paper. Now let's continue.

2. Put the number 8 in the box of the athlete directly above the fencer.
3. Put the number 5 in the box of the athlete in the lower right-hand corner of the page.
4. Put the number 9 in the box of the athlete between the boxer and the soccer player.
5. Put the number 1 in the box of the athlete in the upper right-hand corner of the page.
6. Put the number 12 in the box of the athlete directly to the right of the fencer.
7. Put the number 6 in the box of the athlete directly above the tennis player.
8. Put the number 15 in the box of the athlete in the lower left-hand corner of the page.
9. Put the number 11 in the box of the athlete in the upper left-hand corner of the page.
10. Put the number 2 in the box of the athlete directly to the left of the fencer.
11. Put the number 7 in the box of the athlete directly to the right of the soccer player.
12. Put the number 4 in the box of the athlete directly above the golfer.
13. Put the number 10 in the box of the athlete directly to the right of the ice skater.
14. Put the number 13 in the box of the athlete directly to the left of the golfer.
15. Put the number 14 in the box of the athlete directly below the ice hockey player.
16. Put the number 3 in the box of the athlete directly to the right of the golfer.

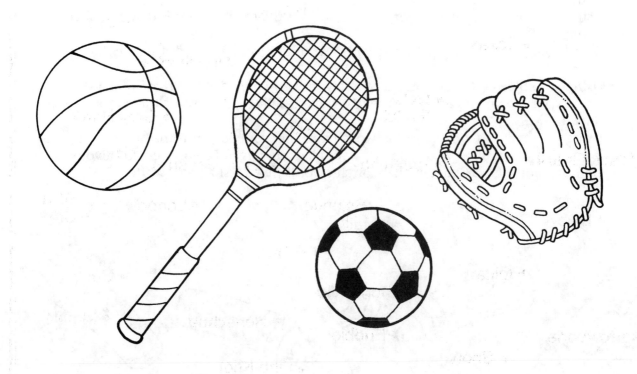

Following Directions • 5–6 ©2004 Creative Teaching Press

Kentucky Towns

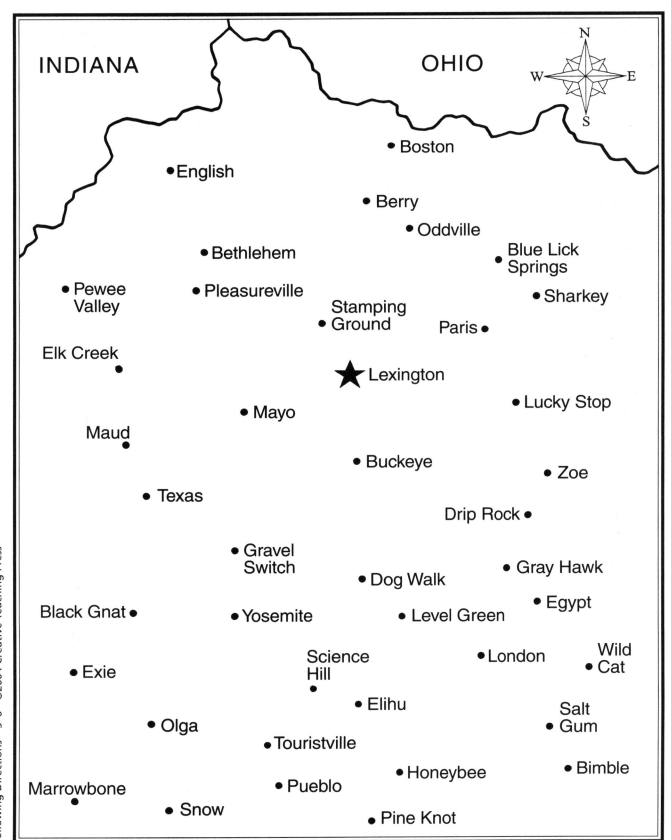

INDIANA

OHIO

N
W   E
S

• Boston

• English

• Berry

• Oddville

Blue Lick
• Springs

• Bethlehem

• Pewee
Valley

• Pleasureville

• Sharkey

Stamping
• Ground

Paris •

Elk Creek
•

★ Lexington

• Lucky Stop

• Mayo

Maud
•

• Buckeye

• Zoe

• Texas

Drip Rock •

• Gravel
Switch

• Gray Hawk

Black Gnat •

• Yosemite

• Level Green

• Egypt

• Exie

Science
Hill
•

• London

Wild
• Cat

• Elihu

Salt
• Gum

• Olga

• Touristville

Marrowbone
•

• Pueblo

• Honeybee

• Bimble

• Snow

• Pine Knot

Name: _____

Western Quest

Washington

Montana

Oregon

Idaho

Wyoming

California

Nevada

Utah

Colorado

Arizona

New Mexico

Following Directions • 5–6 ©2004 Creative Teaching Press

Name: _____

Map of the United States

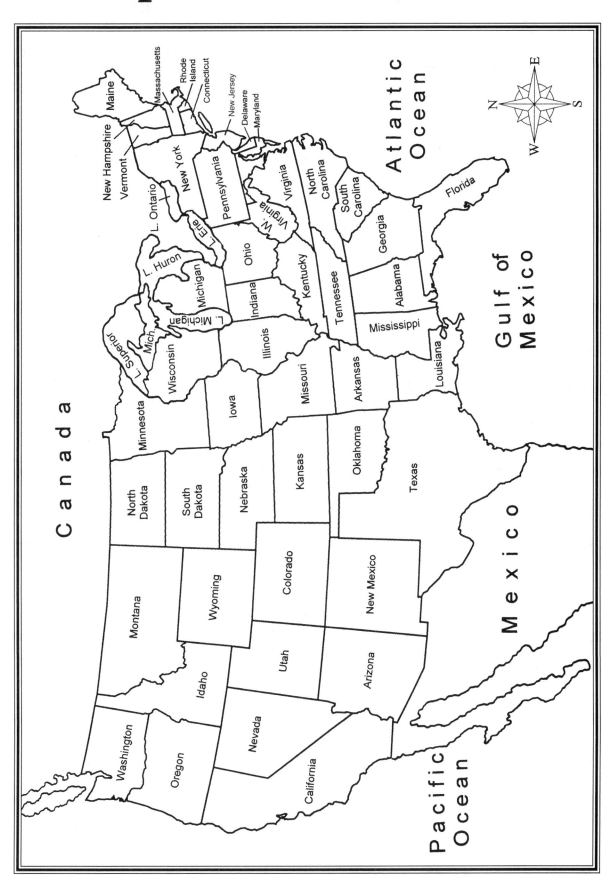

North, South, East, and West

1. _____
2. _____
3. _____
4. _____
5. _____
6. _____
7. _____
8. _____
9. _____
10. _____
11. _____
12. _____

The United States of America

Following Directions • 5–6   ©2004 Creative Teaching Press

Name: _____

In-Between States

1. _____
2. _____
3. _____
4. _____
5. _____
6. _____
7. _____
8. _____
9. _____
10. _____
11. _____
12. _____

Number, Please

1. _____
2. _____
3. _____
4. _____
5. _____
6. _____
7. _____
8. _____
9. _____
10. _____
11. _____
12. _____

Following Directions • 5–6 ©2004 Creative Teaching Press

Hidden Picture #1

Name: _____

Hidden Picture #2

Following Directions • 5–6   ©2004 Creative Teaching Press

The Number Game

10	**24**	**100**	**6**
9	**360**	**4**	**50**
16	**7**	**3**	**12**
60	**5**		
13	**365**		

Customize the Sport Shoes

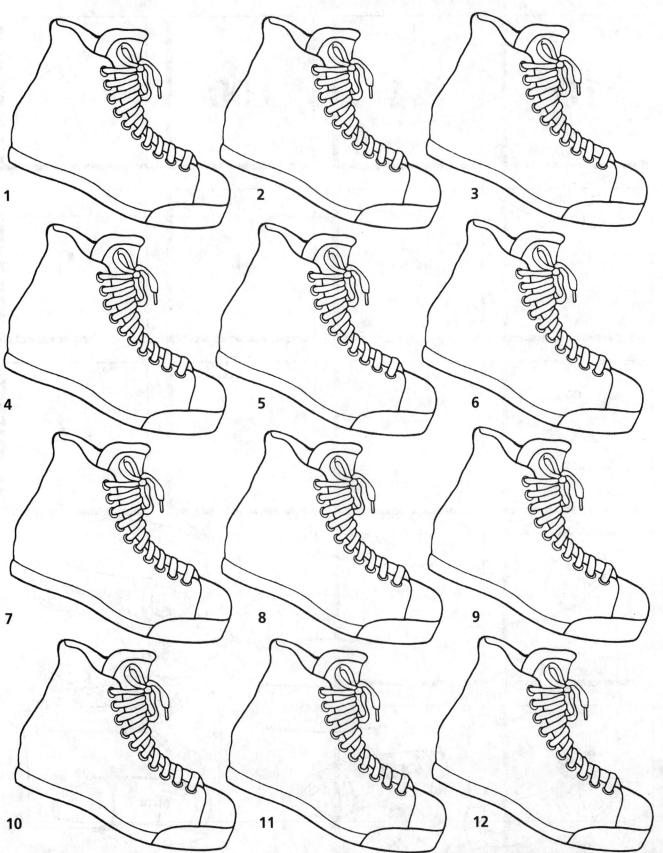

1

2

3

4

5

6

7

8

9

10

11

12

Following Directions • 5–6   ©2004 Creative Teaching Press

Name: _____

Colorful Crayons

Name: _____

Athletes on Parade

Following Directions • 5–6 ©2004 Creative Teaching Press

Answer Key

Page 11: Animal Groups
a clowder of cats
a skulk of foxes
a rafter of turkeys
a gaggle of geese
a colony of rabbits
a troop of kangaroos
a covey of partridges
a muster of peacocks

Page 13: Animal Offspring
kangaroo: joey
ostrich: chick
rhinoceros: calf
eagle: eaglet
otter: whelp
swan: cygnet
turkey: poult
goose: gosling

Page 15: Name the Inventor
helicopter: Igor Sikorsky
hydroplane: Glenn Curtiss
bicycle: James Starley
bifocal lenses: Benjamin Franklin

Page 16: State Safari
The name of the state is Delaware.

Page 18: Name the President
The president who is pictured on the
$5000 bill is James Madison.

Page 20: Geometry Goulash

1. P	10. K, T
2. O	11. L, U, M, F
3. J	12. C
4. G	13. J, O
5. E	14. A
6. S	15. L, U, M, F, E, D
7. N	16. W, H
8. I	17. L, C, A, S, U, M, F, D
9. B	18. C, I, J

Page 22: What's for Dinner?
10, turkey

Page 24: Mall Maze
34

Page 26: Best in Show
The dog the judges picked for Best in Show was the Australian Shepherd.

Page 28: The Magic Number
The magic number is 302,186.

Page 52: Western Quest
Washington: Dusty, George
Oregon: Fossil, Remote
California: Weed, Elk
Idaho: Santa, Riddle
Nevada: Steamboat, Stagecoach
Utah: Bluebell, Sandy
Arizona: Blue, Why
Montana: Fishtail, Pony
Wyoming: Bill, Story
Colorado: Rifle, Brush
New Mexico: Pep, House

Page 54: North, South, East, and West
1. Maine
2. Utah
3. Nebraska
4. Montana
5. North Carolina
6. Florida
7. Nevada
8. Missouri
9. New York
10. Illinois
11. New Mexico
12. Tennessee

Page 55: In-Between States
1. Oklahoma
2. South Dakota
3. Indiana
4. Alabama
5. Iowa
6. Massachusetts
7. Idaho
8. Colorado
9. Ohio
10. Minnesota
11. Mississippi
12. Kentucky

Page 56: Number, Please
1. 4
2. 6
3. 4
4. 1
5. 3
6. 10
7. 6
8. 4
9. 8
10. 6
11. 5
12. 3

Page 59: The Number Game
The number is 4.

Page 61: Colorful Crayons
1. red: ruby, scarlet
2. yellow: canary, goldenrod
3. purple: plum, violet
4. orange: apricot, pumpkin
5. green: olive, emerald
6. blue: cobalt, navy
7. brown: beige, khaki
8. gray: charcoal, taupe
9. white: ivory, alabaster

Page 62: Athletes on Parade
archer: 11
basketball player: 8
runner: 4
bowler: 1
boxer: 2
fencer: 13
golfer: 12
ice hockey player: 3
ice skater: 9
racquetball player: 10
football player: 6
baseball player: 14
soccer player: 15
swimmer: 7
tennis player: 16
weight lifter: 5

Following Directions • 5–6   ©2004 Creative Teaching Press